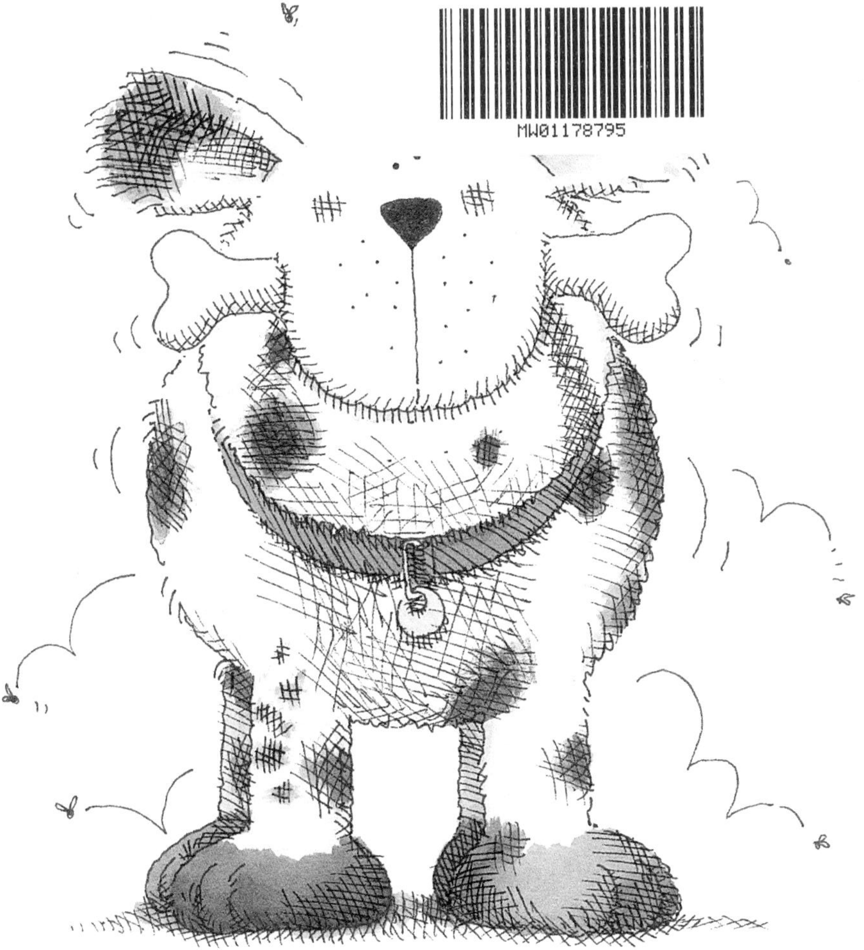

When my dog got dirty,

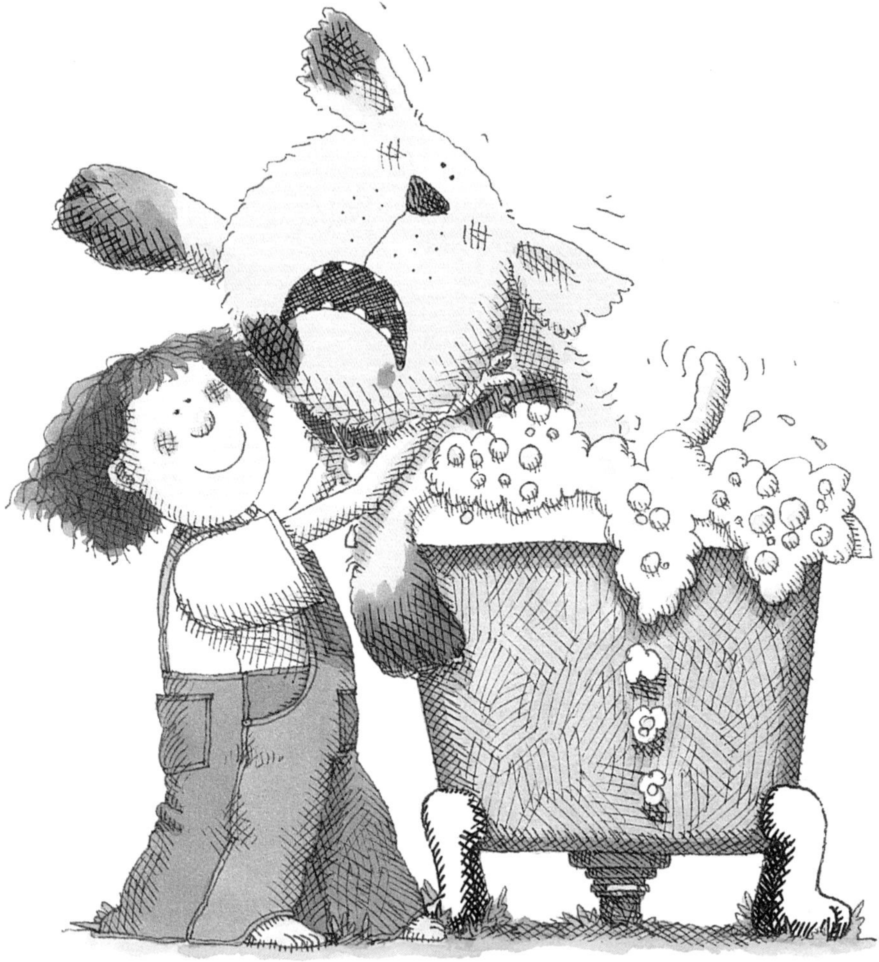

I gave her a bath.

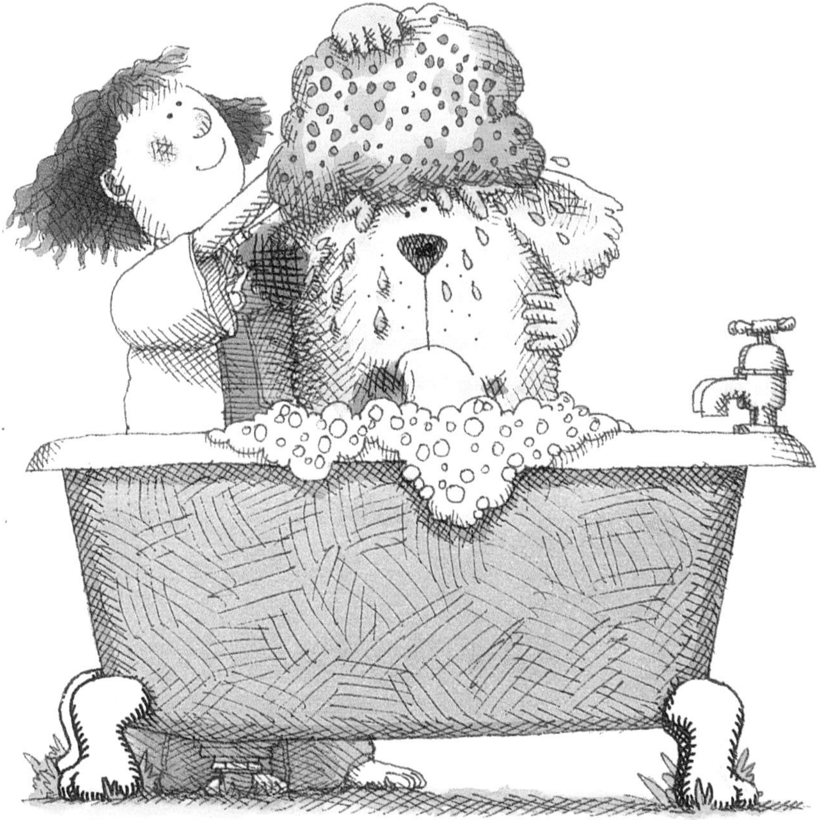

First I wet her,

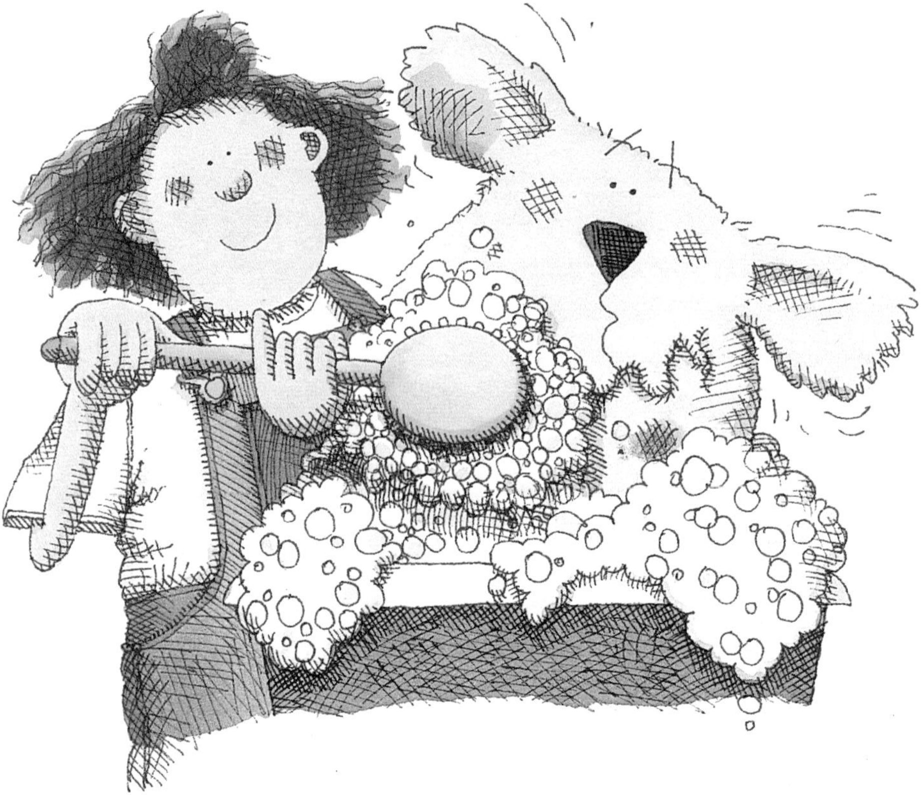

then I washed her.

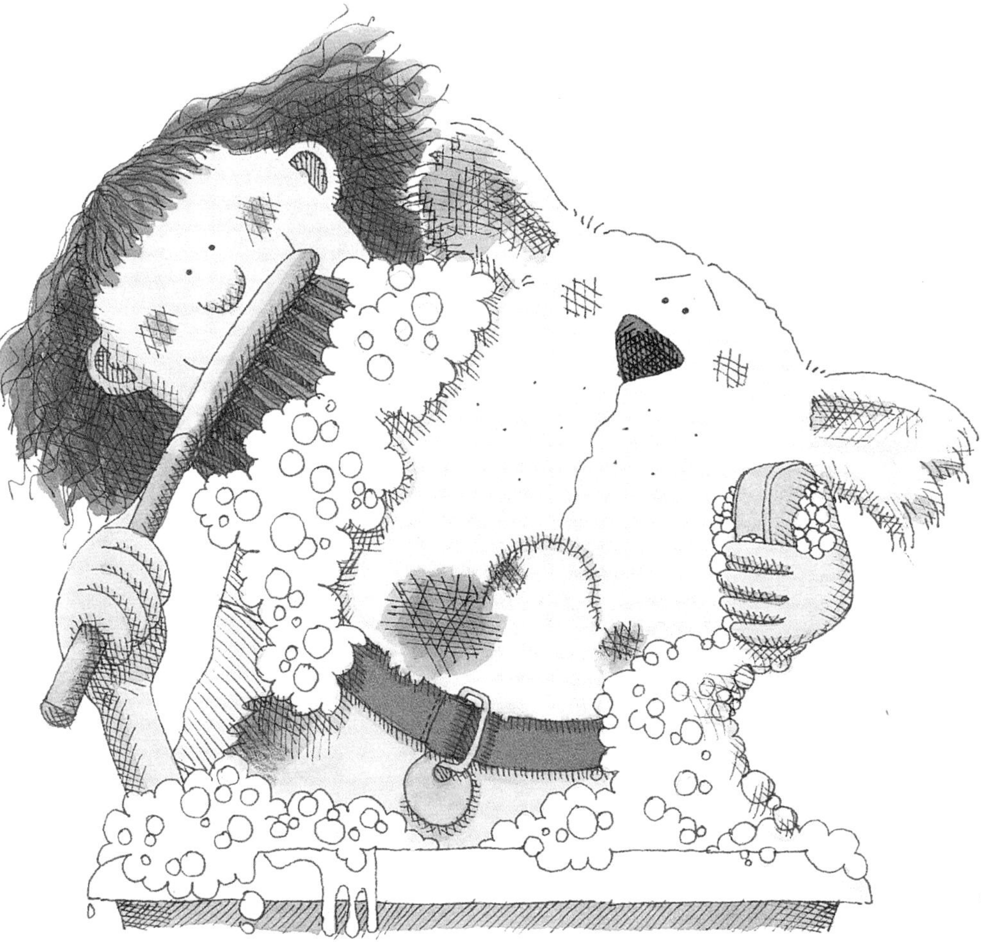

She didn't like it!

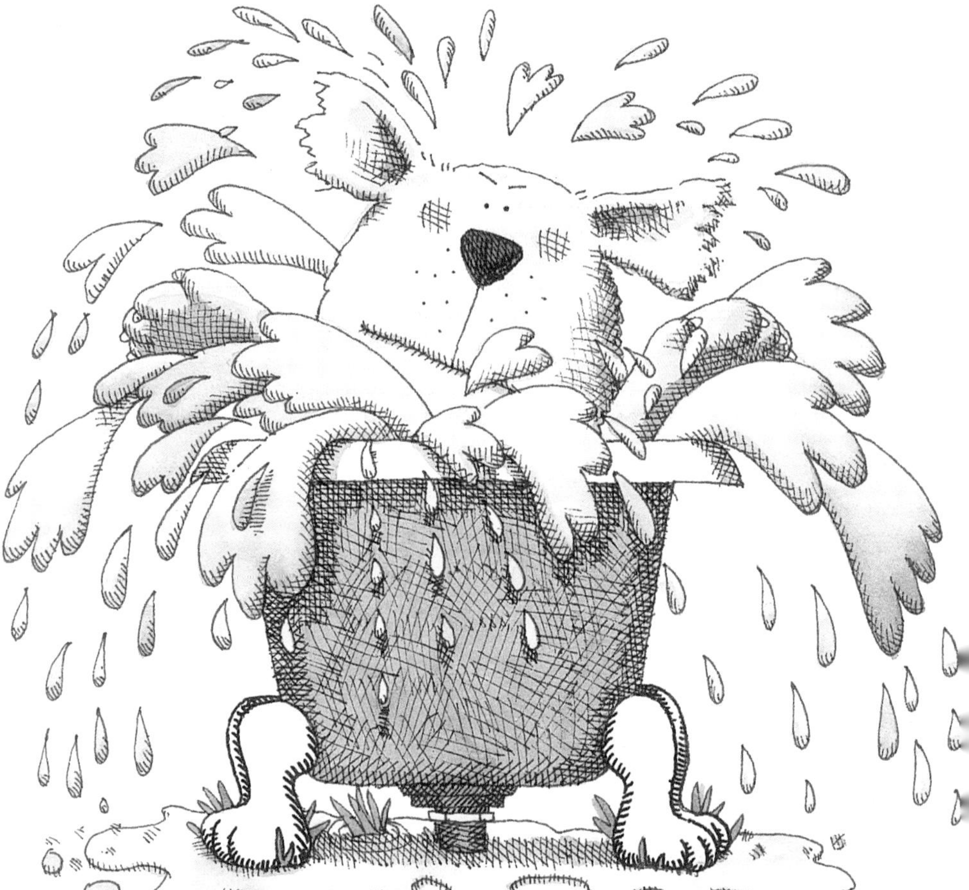

She kicked and she splashed.

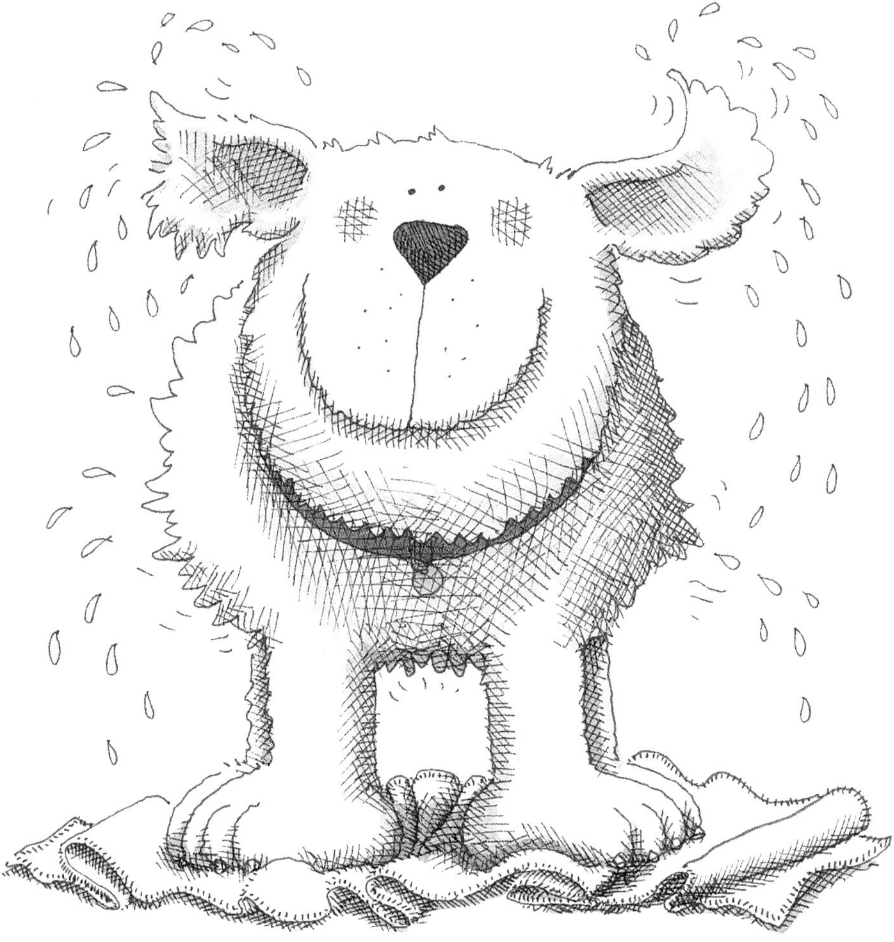

My dog is nice and clean now.

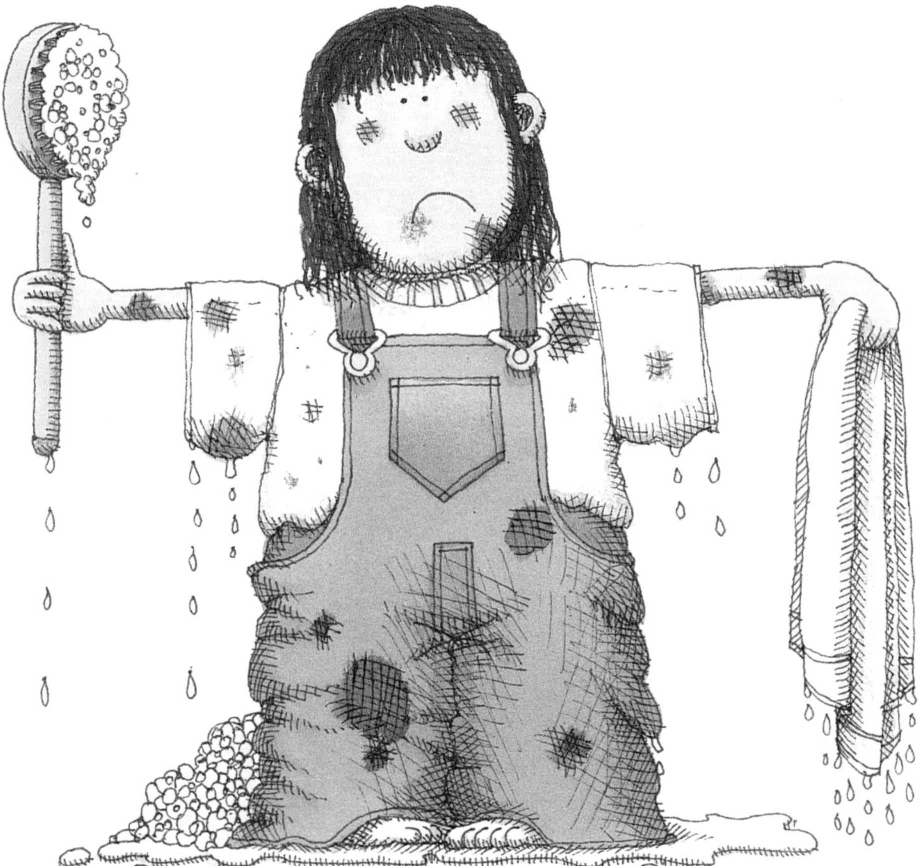

But look at me!